Windows, Memorials, and More

All Saints Episcopal Church
Jensen Beach, Florida

Joyce A. Fletcher Menard

"Windows, Memorials, and More" by Joyce A. Fletcher Menard. ISBN 978-1-62137-181-6 (softcover), 978-1-62137-182-3 (ebook).

Published 2013 by Virtualbookworm.com Publishing Inc., P.O. Box 9949, College Station, TX 77842, US. ©2013, Joyce A. Fletcher Menard. All rights reserved. No part of this publication may be reproduced, stored in a retrieval system, or transmitted in any form or by any means, electronic, mechanical, recording or otherwise, without the prior written permission of Joyce A. Fletcher Menard.

Manufactured in the United States of America.

Dedication

As I was raised in this parish from the late 1950s – until the 1970s, I knew many of the people in the windows and have witnessed many of the changes depicted. I am grateful for the legacy these people gave this community and for the service they gave our Lord. For the encouragement and assistance of many, living and dead, I am forever grateful. It is to all those saints of my parish family, that I dedicate this effort.

Acknowledgements

I am deeply indebted to Sandra Henderson Thurlow, Janet Kempf Siddons, and Ed Pettit for their research and writings. Many thanks to Bob Dobens whose photographs make these stories come to life. The financial support of the Episcopal Church Women was a great blessing and vote of confidence I greatly appreciate. I am grateful to all those unknowable people who filed and maintained the references included in this effort as they kept such great stories. To my Rector, the Rev. W. Frisby Hendricks, III, 7th Rector of All Saints Episcopal Church, I am indebted. Without his editorial assistance, his permission to access the Parish records and his persistence in keeping me focused, this book would not have changed from an idea into the reality you now are reading. Without the patient support of my husband Philip R. Menard and the help of my lifelong friend Mary McGowan Harden, I would never have had the courage to publish this work.

Foreword

My purpose is to share what is known about the windows and some of the memorials, the people who are remembered, and the donors. Former member and stained glass aficionado, Edward Petit researched the windows for the Parish's 100th Anniversary celebration. Unfortunately, his work was available for a brief year and then was filed in the parish office. In 2009, All Saints Episcopal Church was featured in the Annual Historic Homes and Buildings Tour, coordinated by Stuart Heritage, Inc. The research in preparation for the docent's presentation for that event and subsequent tours serves as the basis of this book.

None of these are Tiffany stained glass as carefully researched by Mr. Petit. Unless otherwise specified, the glass studios are unknown based upon review of the windows and documentation available. The windows are sequenced chronologically and by family connections to facilitate the telling of the history. A diagram of the window locations is provided for the convenience of those who enter. A glossary is found in the back.

Please know that not everything is known or knowable about this historic building. The author requests any errors or additional information be brought to her attention in order that this history be as thorough and accurate as possible in future editions.

Joyce A. FLetcher Menard

Church Window Locations

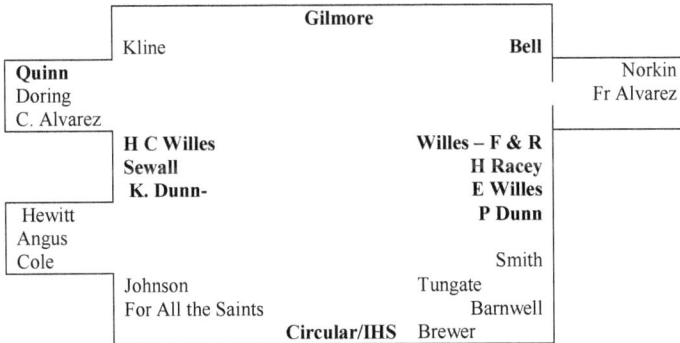

	Gilmore		
Kline		Bell	Norkin
Quinn			Fr Alvarez
Doring			
C. Alvarez			
H C Willes	**Willes – F & R**		
Sewall	**H Racey**		
K. Dunn-	**E Willes**		
Hewitt	**P Dunn**		
Angus			
Cole	Smith		
Johnson	Tungate		
For All the Saints	Barnwell		
Circular/IHS	Brewer		

Bold Print indicates pre-WWI Windows
The Hewitt/Angus/Cole windows are located in the original entry.
The Brewer windows are in the current main entry. HIS window is in the choir loft
Norkin and Fr. Alvarez windows are in the sacristy and not visible from inside the church

The History

All Saints continues to serve God as a testimony to the faith and dedication of the members down through the decades. History, beauty and a patina of prayer surround all who enter.

The founding community of Episcopalians is first recorded in the published diary of the Bishop of the Missionary Diocese of Southern Florida, the Rt. Rev. William Crane Gray, when he visited in 1893. At the time, this area was known as Waveland and was in Brevard County.

Charles H. Racey and his wife, Mary, donated the land for the church and cemetery. Charles led the fund raising effort as treasurer. Built in 1898, and dedicated one year later, the church is the oldest in Martin County, Florida.

The church had seventeen original windows. Fourteen survived until the 1950s. All that is known about those three windows are the names of the donors and in whose memory they were given.

The history of the church's memorials discussed here is reflected primarily in two time periods; the 1890s through the 1930s and 1950s to 2011. The church became self-sufficient in 1960 and was admitted to the Diocese of South Florida as a parish. In 1963, the building was moved from the original site on this hilltop to the current location to allow for growth. As membership grew, the building was expanded in 1979 and again in 1994. All of these events and changes in worship practices, generated modification to the structure, interior design, the addition of nine windows and the use of the space.

circa 1950s

circa 1977

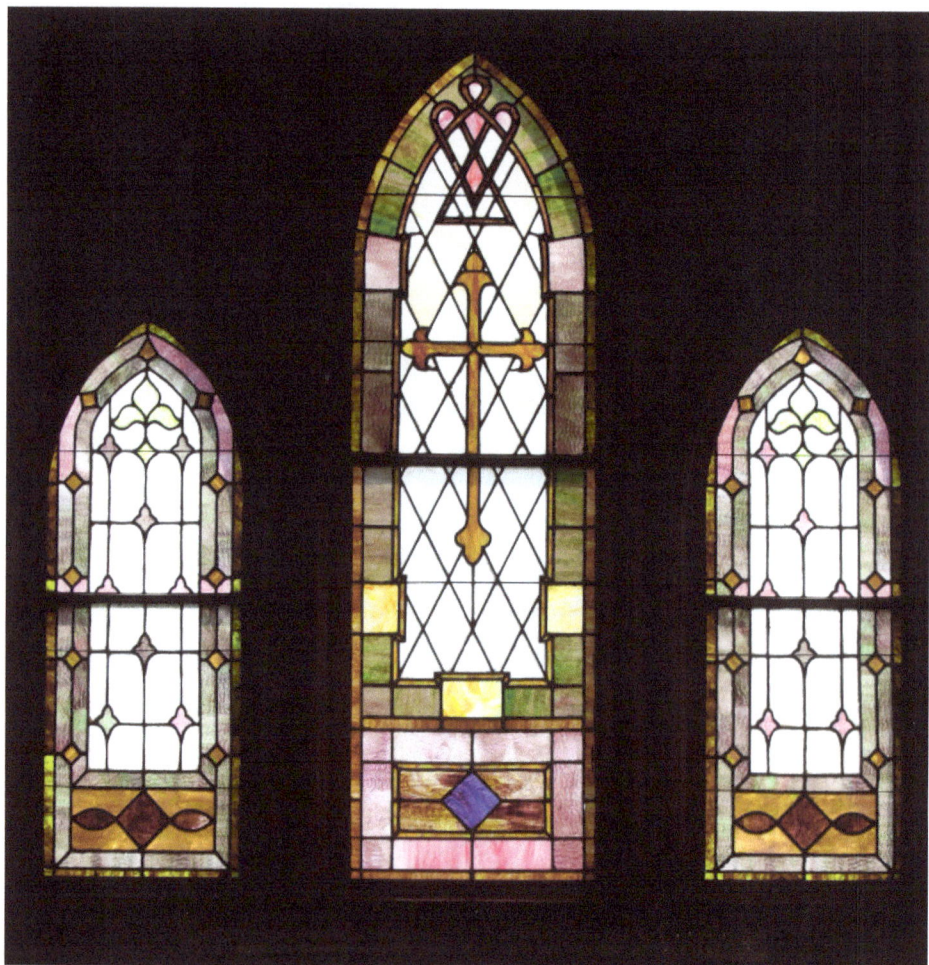

Gilmore Windows

The three windows, behind the altar on the eastern wall serve as a memorial to the Rev. John Gilmore, Rector of Woodham Mortimer, Essex, England. The Rev. Gilmore died in 1897 as shown on the memorial plaque below the windows. The Rev. Gilmore's son, Walter G. Gilmore was the first senior warden of All Saints Episcopal Church. Viewers are reminded of the Holy Trinity because there are three windows, which form a gothic arch and a perfect triangle. Made by an unknown glass company circa 1926, they are original windows. In the Diocesan Bishop's diary on February 23, 1900, "Mr. Gilmore is noted as a lay reader who did good work, ..." The Parish Register records that Mr. Gilmore returned to England.

Isabel Kline

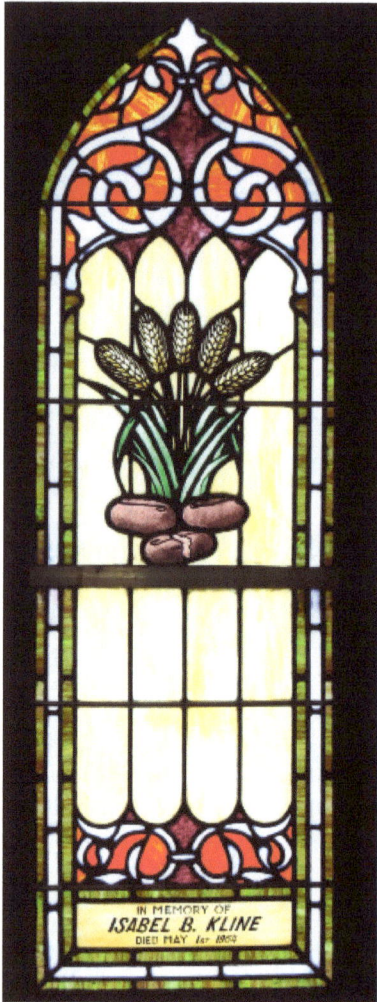

The Rector, Vestry and people of All Saints gave this window in thanksgiving for Isabel B. Kline who died May 1, 1964 in Vero Beach, Florida. Mrs. Andrew (Alice) Carnegie donated the original window in this space. This replacement window depicts a sheaf of wheat and loaves of bread, symbolic of the Body of Christ in the Holy Communion. The K. J. Mueller Studios of Zephyrhills, Florida crafted this window circa 1965. Isabel taught school in Sebastian, Florida. She died at the age of 63, had no survivors, and was not on the church membership rolls. Isabel Kline left $15,000 to the church for use at the discretion of the Rector. Among other improvements, these funds provided for the installation of air conditioning; a vast improvement over having screened windows and using hand held fans in the tropical heat.

Thomas and Jane Dewart Bell

Mrs. William (Alice) Carnegie gave this window in memory of her parents, Thomas and Jane Dewart Bell. The grapes and chalice depicted represent the wine of Holy Communion as the Blood of Christ. This window was crafted circa 1925. The Bells were not members here, nor were they buried here. Their daughter, Alice, wed William Carnegie, a nephew of Andrew Carnegie the famous industrialist and philanthropist. Thomas died before he saw his daughter married. "The New York Times" reported that the Carnegie family professed to know nothing of the affair or the bride. The newly wed Mr. & Mrs. William Carnegie, wintered with Mrs. Bell after their wedding. Subsequently, the couple established an estate known as Lucindia on nearby Sewall's Point, Florida.

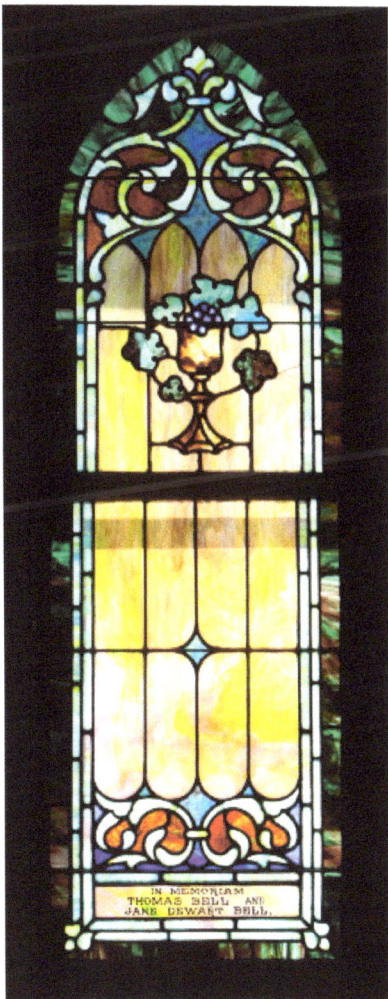

Helen Catherine Racey

This memorial to Helen Catherine Racey, who died March 31, 1880, depicts a descending dove representing the Holy Spirit. This window was created circa 1925. Mrs. Racey was not a member of All Saints and is not recorded as being buried here. Her son, Charles, gave the initial property for the church and cemetery and was probably the donor; Helen was his mother, though no documentation of the donor has been found. Parish records show Charles, wife Mary, and their family moved to Dade County, Florida.

Edith Alston Willes

Edith Alston Willes died May 1, 1880. Her son, Frederick W. Willes is the probable donor, though no documentation has been found. Mrs. Willes was not a member of All Saints and is not recorded as being buried here. Symbolic of eternal life, three endless ribbons are shown in the top, middle and center of this window. A deep purple Bishop's mitre pays tribute to the GGGG Great Uncle of the Willes children, the Right Reverend Edward Willes. In 1773, at the age of 80, Bishop Willes died and was interred in Westminster Abbey. An unknown American glass company, circa 1925, made this window. Old photographs show that this window was originally on the back wall of the church. The window was placed in this location after the church was moved in 1963. What this window replaced is unknown.

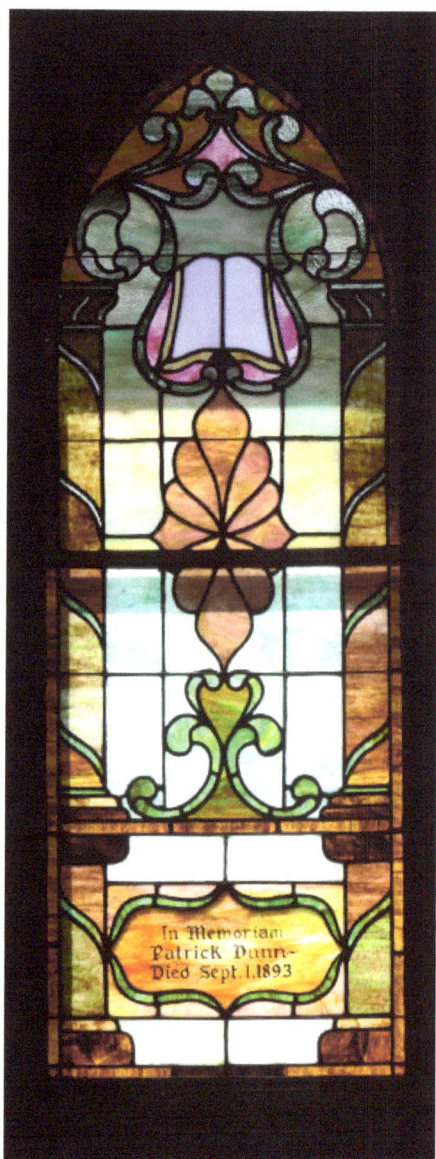

Katherine and Patrick Dunn

Mr. and Mrs. Dunn were the parents of Mrs. Frederick (Elizabeth) Willes and Mrs. Charles (Mary) Racey; the maternal grandparents of the Willes and Racey children. These windows were made by an unknown American glass studio, circa 1925, and are some of the original windows.

Though there is no documentation on the donors, one would reasonably guess that the Willes and/or Racey family paid for these windows. One is a memorial to Katherine (nee Dundon) Dunn, who died August 1, 1888. This Latin cross with a king's crown is symbolic of eternal life. This window was originally installed on the back wall, under the Rose circular window and next to Edith Alston Willes' window. This window was moved to this location after the church was moved in 1963. What this window replaced is unknown.

The other window is a memorial to Patrick Dunn who died September 1, 1893. The open book is symbolic of the Holy Bible. The Dunns died prior to the construction of the church, after their daughters had left England for America.

Frieda and Richard Willes

Created circa 1925, this window is an abstract depiction of two cherubs. No documentation has been found on this memorial to Frieda Mary Willes (May 17, 1906 – December 31, 1906) and Richard Alston Willes (October 1907 - 1 December 1907). Their parents, Elizabeth (nee Dunn) and Frederick W. Willes are the probable donors; no documentation has been found. Frieda was baptized in extremis by her father, as no clergy were available. She died of typhoid and her brother Richard died of pneumonia. Their parents and some of their siblings are buried with these infants in the All Saints Cemetery. Mr. Willes was the first Junior Warden and then Senior Warden for many years.

Harry Charles Willes

This window depicts a chalice, and was created circa 1925. A memorial to Harry Charles Willes, this window probably was given by his parents, Elizabeth (nee Dunn) and Frederick W. Willes, though no documentation has been found. Harry died at the age of 13 on November 8, 1918, while climbing a fence with a loaded shotgun, which accidentally discharged. He was the third of the Willes children who did not reach adulthood. Harry Charles was named for his paternal grandfather Willes, an Anglican cleric who is well documented in the records of the Church of England.

Henry E. Sewall

As Captain Henry E. Sewall was a merchant marine, the symbol of the anchor is quite fitting for this memorial window. The anchor has great importance to mariners and was regarded in ancient times as a symbol of safety. When adopted by Christians, the anchor became a symbol of hope. Henry E. Sewall survived a shipwreck while serving on his uncle's ship as a young man. Later in life, Henry established the post office on Sewall's Point, Florida and developed that portion of what today is Martin County, Florida. Born on August 22, 1848, in St. Augustine, Florida, he died in Daytona, Florida on August 1, 1925. His wife and sister succeeded him in death and are the likely donors of this window, which was created circa 1925. He, his wife Abbie Evans Sewall, and his sister Anna, are all buried in All Saints Cemetery. Henry was the Great Great Uncle of current parishioner Karen (Smith) Neff, by Henry's sister Elizabeth (Sewall) Smith.

14

Marian D. Beardsley Quinn

The choice of white lilies indicates purity and freedom from sin through Jesus' death on the cross. This is a memorial to Marian Dorothea Beardsley Quinn. Circa 1926, this was the third of the windows Mrs. William (Alice) Carnegie donated. The connection between Mrs. Carnegie and Mrs. Quinn is unknown. This window was originally installed here as is described in the parish service record book on April 26, 1931. Dying at the age of 25, she was the mother of two boys, Harper and Albert. Mrs. Quinn is buried in the All Saints Cemetery. Her grave is marked with a very large headstone, easily visible from the southern cemetery road in the original part of the cemetery.

15

The Tyndall Plaque

Mr. and Mrs. E.C.B. Tyndall gave this brass plaque found on the wall to the left side of the altar. The plaque commemorates their second and third sons, both of whom died while on active duty. The Tyndall family was among the founding members, and their sons received the sacrament of confirmation here.

Frances B. "Frank" Tyndall was a World War I pilot. He served overseas; most notably in the largest assembly of combat aviation assets ever seen during World War I. Between the two World Wars, Frank was killed when his military aircraft crashed in July 1930, leaving a wife and young daughter. Tyndall U.S. Air Force Base, near Panama Beach, Florida, was named in his honor in the 1940s. As an adult, his daughter is known to visit the area and occasionally stops in to the church.

Bruce A. Tyndall arrived at Maxwell Field, Alabama in 1929, was on the base polo team, and quickly married. The plaque states that Bruce was married on December 22, 1931, and that Bruce died a year and a day later. Newspaper articles reported he was taking one of his soldiers home for the holidays, when his aircraft crashed. The family moved from the area and none of the family is recorded as being buried at All Saints Cemetery.

Prayer Desk and Lectern

On the letterhead of R.C. Geissler, Inc., New York, New York, there was a note from March 6, 1928, acknowledging the order of this prayer bench and lectern. They were "completed in half the usual time", so that the congregation could utilize these items on Easter. They have a hand rubbed, weathered oak oil finish, and were paid in full by August of that year at a total cost of $156. The shipping cost was $11.

There were two donors. One donor was the Stuart Lodge #152, Fraternal Order of Knights of Pythias; an international fraternity, founded in 1864. This organization promotes peace through understanding. Prior to the establishment of St. Mary's Episcopal Church in Stuart, Florida, there was an Episcopal community. The Episcopal Guild, the women's group from Stuart contributed the balance. In the letter bearing the guild's check, the secretary wrote, the group "will appreciate having the prayer desk marked as a gift of the guild." The ladies' request has not been honored.

The Rose Window

The letters I H S displayed in the circular rose window has several traditions connected with their use: as an abbreviation of the name Jesus in Greek, as the Latin phrase Jesus Hominum Salvator (Jesus, Savior of Men), and as the German phrase Heiland, Seligmacher (Jesus, Lord, Savior). There is growing popularity in I H S being an abbreviation for the phrase "In His Service." The name of the donor and the American glass company are both unknown for this window made before 1925. Still set in the original location, this window was repaired with some of the Kline Estate funds. It has survived the move and two subsequent expansions of the building.

Visionary Years - 1950s & 1960s

In the 1950s, the church property was initially expanded with the donation of a lot from Lydia and A. A. "Buck" Hendry and another from Nathan and Clara Gilman, and with the purchase of three lots from Sarah and David Rosser in 1958. At the dead end of Sea View Road, a cottage was built in 1954 to house temporary clergy who served the congregation. A young Vicar Purdom sought and received the dead end of Sea View Road from the Martin County Commission. The Rosser property included a house, which became the vicarage and rectory until 1966.

In the 1960s, that early cottage was moved, and became the Patrician Street entrance for the parish hall. Named Houg Hall after Vestryman Carl Houg, the parish hall was dedicated on All Saints Day, 1960. To allow for a growing congregation and community, in the summer of 1963, the church was moved to the adjoining Rosser and Hendry lots. A new entry was established to the church building.

The Rosser house is shown to the left in the black and white photo on the following page, depicting the laying of the cornerstone in October 1963.

Top Left: The 1963 Move. **Top Right:** Summer 1964.
Bottom: Dedication by the Rev. Norman B. Feaster, 2nd Rector, and the Vestry in Octoober 1963. The building on the left is the Rectory 1959 - 1966

Change

When the church was moved, the original entry was no longer practical, since that entry was now facing the cemetery. A new entrance was created as is shown on the previous page.

The original vestibule was converted into the baptistery, where the marble baptismal font was then placed. The font was given by Mrs. Herbert Taylor and blessed by Bishop Co-Adjutor John D. Wing, on his visit of June 10, 1926. Connie Segerstrom Haire was baptized in this font, in 1927, and still worships here at the time of this publication. Three windows with a baptism theme were installed in the new baptistery, using this font, and are described in the following pages.

Subsequently, the font was moved to the exterior under the Alleluia Cross for a period.

Doris and Richard Angus

This window depicts three fish in a circle surrounded by the words, "I baptize thee in the Name of the Father, and the Son, and the Holy Ghost." An unknown glass studio created this window, circa 1966. Doris gave this window. Richard Gorham "Dick" Angus, was a native of Albany, NY, and a retired manager for Prudential Life Insurance. A resident here for 29 years, Dick was a member of the World War I Barracks #854, but was not a church member. At age 91, he died in Stuart, Florida and was buried in Albany, New York. He and Doris had no children.

Doris was a faithful member who aged gracefully, participating as long as someone would bring her to church and her health would allow, until her death in 1993. There is no record that she is buried in All Saints Cemetery.

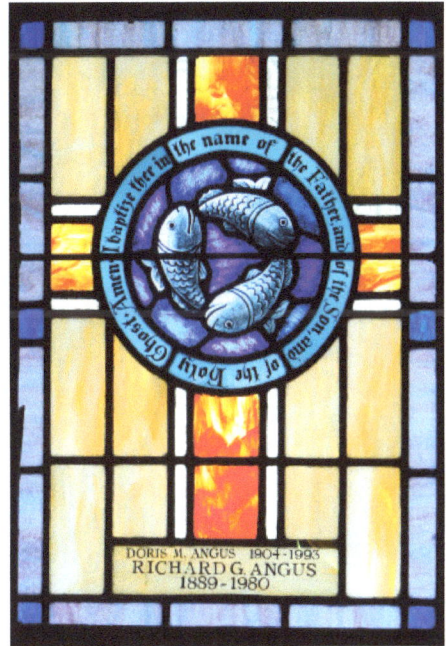

Alma and Joseph Cole

This window portrays Jesus with the descending dove, representing the Holy Spirit as described in scripture. Created by the Wippell Mowbray Studio, circa 1995, Joseph Cole purchased the window. A native of Newport, Rhode Island, his wife Alma Rene, was an executive assistant in a local bank. Later, she was the owner of Alma's Fashion Fabrics. She was one of the first two women elected to the Vestry. Alma served on the Altar Guild and was involved with the establishment of the church's thrift shop by the Episcopal Church Women. Alma died May 18, 2002, at the age of 78 in Stuart, Florida.

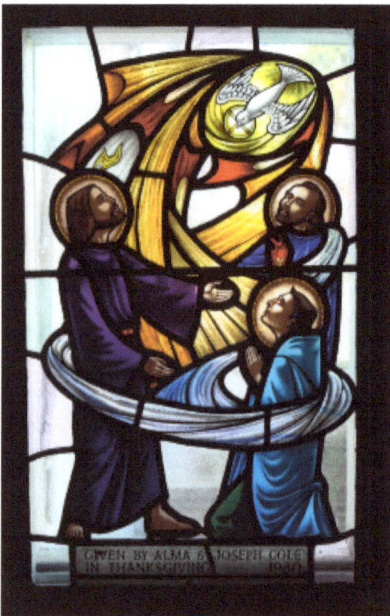

A native of Washington, D.C., her husband Joe, served in the Coast Guard during World War II and was a letter carrier for the U.S. Postal Service for 20 years. At the age of 83, Joe died February 29, 2004. Married for more than 60 years, they are buried in All Saints Cemetery.

Francis and Walter Hewitt

This window is another interpretation of John baptizing our Lord. Created by an unknown glass company circa 1980, Walter Hewitt purchased this window as a memorial to his wife, Francis. The couple came from Grand Rapids, Michigan in 1962. Francis Clark Hewitt was a native of Oshkosh, Wisconsin, who died in Stuart, Florida, at age 79 in September 1979. Fran was involved with the Episcopal Church Women's group.

Walter was born in Kenosha, Wisconsin, served in World War I and was a personnel manager for 27 years. Walter was on the Bishop's Committee during the mission years, and subsequently the Vestry. He served as the church treasurer and was also involved with the cemetery. Walter was 88 when he died on Valentine's Day, 1986. There were no children; only a nephew is known to survive him.

IN MEMORY OF
1891-HENRY DORING-1975
1893-JOSEPHINE F. DORING-1986

Henry and Josephine Doring

In this window are trumpets, which are symbolic of the call for the resurrection of the dead. A stained glass studio created this window, circa 1966, at the request of Josephine Doring, who purchased this window. Henry Doring, 84, died on Christmas, 1975 in Stuart, Florida. In World War I, he served in the U.S. Army. This native of New York City was a retired bank clerk and a member of the Veterans of World War I, Martin County Barracks #854. In 1962, Henry was appointed to the Bishop's Committee and subsequently served on the Vestry. For many years he was the head usher. Carillon bells were installed in 1975 in his honor.

Unable to safely live alone, his wife "Jo" moved to the Bishop Gray Inn. Located in Davenport, Florida, this church operated senior housing facility was more than two and half hours drive from Jensen Beach, Florida. The women of the church maintained contact with her for many years, occasionally visiting and bringing gifts and comfort items to "Jo" and the residents. The Dorings had no children and are buried together here.

EDWARD GORDON BREWER 1891-1981

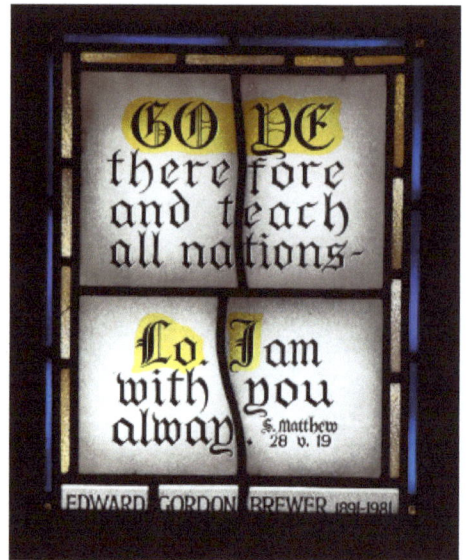

EDWARD GORDON BREWER 1891-1981

Edward Gordon Brewer

Depicted in the entry doors are the words of Matthew 28:19 and a crown with the word "Sanctus", meaning "Holy" in Latin. An unknown glass company, circa 1992, made these windows. These are not in the original doors of the church.

Maureen and Alan Brewer donated the windows to memorialize Alan's brother, Edwin Gordon Brewer. Gordon was born in London, England on May 26, 1891. He came to America, became a U.S. citizen, and registered for the World War I draft at the age of 26. After being discharged from the Coast Guard in 1921, he became a Florida resident and was one of the first property owners and developers on Hutchinson Island, Florida. During World War II, he leased land on Hutchinson Island to the U.S. Coast Guard. Barracks and stables were constructed on that land and used by the Coast Guard during the war. After the war, he transformed those buildings into an inn known as the Kensington Club. The women of the church frequently held card parties there before All Saints had a parish hall.

He died June 10, 1981 in Hendersonville, North Carolina, at the age of 90. He is not buried in the All Saints Cemetery. Allen and his wife, Maureen, both, survived Gordon and were members of this church. His life partner predeceased him.

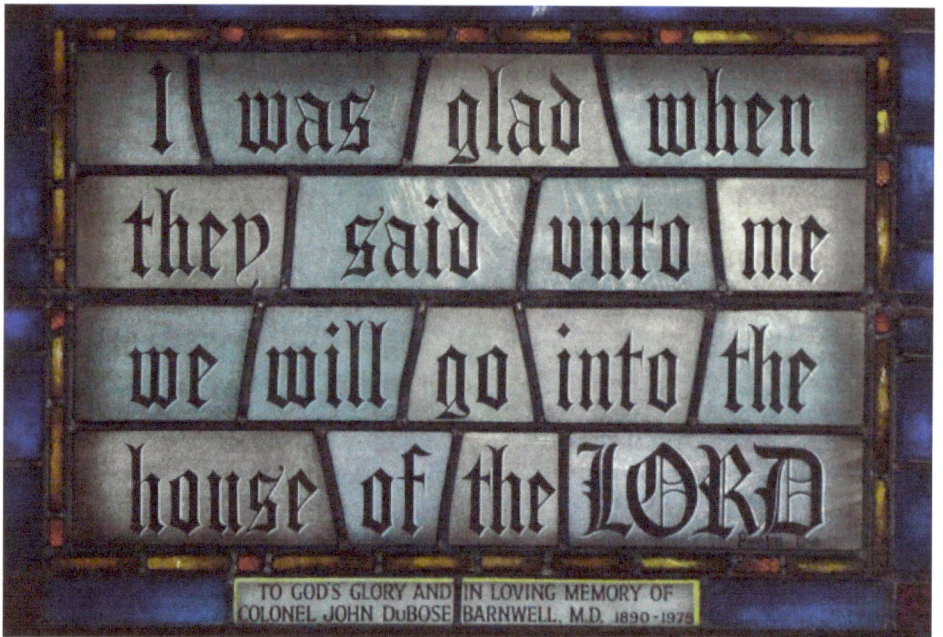

I was glad when they said unto me we will go into the house of the LORD

TO GOD'S GLORY AND IN LOVING MEMORY OF
COLONEL JOHN DuBOSE BARNWELL, M.D. 1890-1975

John DuBose Barnwell

The window has the scripture verse Psalm 122 v.1. This window was added when the church was moved and a new entry added. Colonel Barnwell, U.S. Army (retired), was the Senior Warden when the current site of the church was purchased and he was on the Vestry when the church was moved in 1963. A native of Henderson, Kentucky, he was a veteran of both World Wars and served 30 years in the Army. He was one of the first military flight surgeons in the U.S. Army. He was educated at Sewanee Military Academy, the University of the South at Sewanee Tennessee, at the University of Virginia, and the Army Medical College in Washington, D.C.

He was survived by: his third wife, Alice, and children from a previous wife three daughters, five grandchildren, one great grandchild, two brothers and four sisters. Alice Durkee Barnwell donated this window created by the Wippell Mowbray Studio. Alice was elected to the Vestry along with Alma Cole. A gifted florist, she arranged the flowers for more than 35 years in this church. John was 80 when he married Alice here at All Saints. They celebrated their anniversary every month.

Florence Johnson

The Ten Commandments are depicted in this window crafted circa 1966. The donor of this window, dedicated to Florence Johnson, is unknown. She was a communicant of this church from the 1950s. During the days of our first Rector, Vestry minutes record that Miss or Mrs. Johnson was involved administratively. In 1959, the vestry established her pay at $1/hour for about 3 hours a day. She is pictured in surviving photographs of Christmas bazaars sponsored by the Episcopal Church Women. Florence was born March 31, 1908, and died in Pinellas County, Florida on November 15, 1997. Whether Florence was a spinster, widowed or divorced remains a mystery. Florence's grave is here but cemetery records do not show her as having been interred at All Saints.

Ralph Norkin and Mary Jane Taylor

The symbols of the seven sacraments of the Church are depicted here. At the top, the shell (baptism), the Bishop's mitre (confirmation), the cross and intertwined rings (matrimony), the chalice and bread (Holy Communion), the oil stock (healing), the stole (confession and reconciliation), and the keys (ordination to the holy orders – deacon, priest and bishop.) The Wippell Mowbray Studio created this window circa 1979. Ellen A. Norkin purchased this window in memory of her husband Ralph A. Norkin and her mother in law, Mary Jane Taylor. Ralph A. Norkin died at the age of 65. A native of New York, he was the former Chief Administrator for the Department of Traffic for New York City. They had no children. Nothing more has been found on Ellen's life.

This window is not visible by the congregation as it is located in the sacristy, a small room, located behind the pulpit.

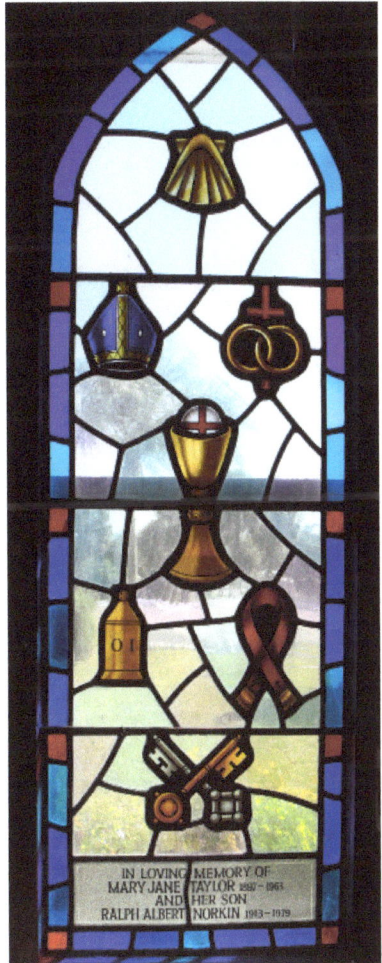

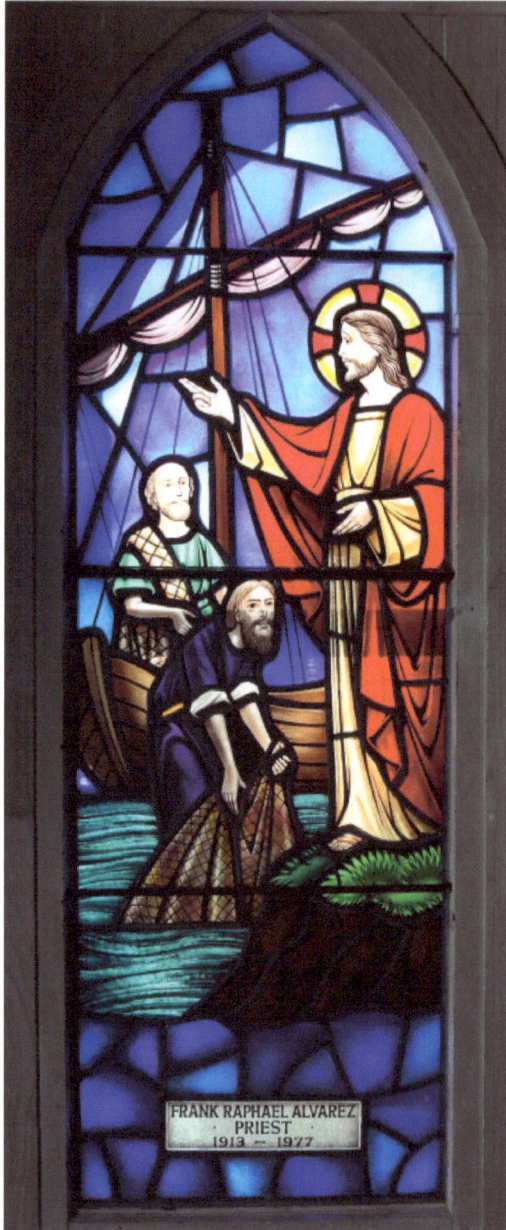

FRANK RAPHAEL ALVAREZ
PRIEST
1913 — 1977

Frank Rafael Alvarez

The Wippell Mowbray Studio made this window with the depiction of Jesus calling the fishermen, Simon Peter and Andrew, to follow him. It is a donation made by the Alvarez family and friends in memory of the Rev. Frank R. Alvarez. This window is not visible by the congregation as it is also located in the sacristy. The location was selected to remind the priests who would prepare for services in this room that they too were called to be fishers of men.

Father Alvarez was installed as the fourth rector of All Saints on February 1, 1970. Born in Tampa, he was a graduate of Carroll College and the Nashotah House Seminary in Nashotah, Wisconsin.

Fr. Alvarez is the only rector to officiate at his daughter's marriage, to die as rector, whose body had lain in state in the church, and was buried from this church. After his death, his daughter, Mary C. Alvarez Rosendahl was ordained a priest in the Episcopal Church. It is believed he would have been pleased.

CELESTE E. ALVAREZ

Celeste Erben Alvarez

In 2010, the Conrad Pickett Studio of Vero Beach, Florida created this depiction of Mary and Jesus, known as Our Lady of Walsingham. This window is the only one commemorating a specific saint. This window is the most ornate. The site for this window was created from what was originally a wall and is best seen by those serving at the Altar. Those sitting in the congregation do not see it. Celeste's devotion to the Blessed Mother and her English lineage influenced the design choice. She was born on April 12, 1923 in Philadelphia, Pennsylvania. In 1970, she came here with the Rev. Frank Alvarez as the rector's wife. Widowed in 1977, at various times she became the parish secretary, the treasurer, the cemetery manager, the LeDuc Scholarship Fund coordinator, and the treasurer for the Episcopal Church Women. She was vital to the thrift shop from the beginning. Celeste's ministry was behind the scenes and seldom seen by the congregation. She died at the age of 87. Survived by her daughter, four sons, eight grandchildren fourteen great-grandchildren, this window was dedicated on December 11, 2011 with many of them present.

Robert James Smith

Maxwell H. and Beulah Frances "Bea" Smith gave this memorial to Robert James Smith (1928 – 1948). Noah's ark is symbolic of hope and salvation. The K.J. Mueller Studios created this window, circa 1966. Nothing is known of Robert. No records of his life have been found. Based upon the dates of his life, he may have been their son or a younger brother.

Parish files and cemetery records tell us only about the donors. "Bea" and "Max" were both members of this church. Bea died in October 1967, was buried in the churchyard, and her grave is marked with an Eastern Star insignia. Max was on the Bishop's Committee, the Vestry and was responsible for the Christian Education Committee in the late 1950s and 1960s. Max's plot in the cemetery is paid for and his name is on their shared headstone, but remains unused. Efforts to find obituaries on Max and Bea were unsuccessful.

Matthew Douglas Tungate

The Wippell Mowbray Studio created the window, circa 1979, depicting Jesus with the children. Donated by the Tungate family, this is a memorial to Matthew Douglas Tungate.

Matthew had only 2 days of life in November 1978. Six new pews at the time of the first expansion were given in memory of Matthew. His parents and grandparents were members here. Matthew's father was a local postman, who served on the Vestry of this parish. This sadness of this infant's death was suffered not only by the Tungate family but the parish family as well. Tungate family members have subsequently been buried along side him in the All Saints Cemetery.

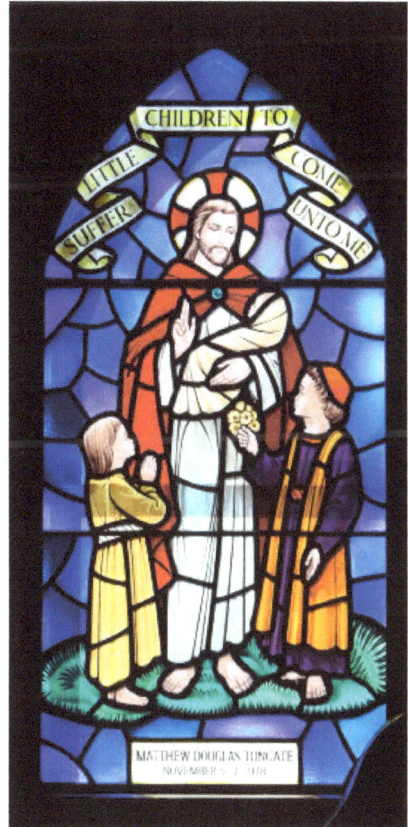

For All The Saints...

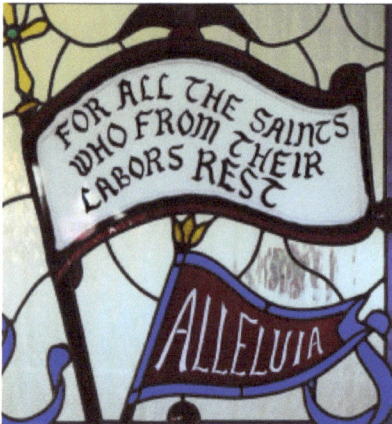

One banner depicted contains the first line of Hymn #297 contained in 1982 Hymnal authorized for use by the Episcopal Church. An unknown American glass company created this window circa 1995. With the second expansion of the building, the Barnwell window had to be re-installed in a new place, and it was determined a companion window was needed. This window was purchased with Building Funds as a memorial to the members of the parish.

The sixth Rector, the Rev. Thomas F. Ryan, Jr. selected this window's design. This is the only window designed by a Rector. The window was installed with the word "their" spelled incorrectly. The window was removed, the error corrected, and the window re-installed. The Rev. Ryan served this congregation longer than any other priest, from 1988 – 2005.

The Altar Kneelers

While her husband battled cancer, Mrs. Edward Smith made the original thirteen-needlepoint kneelers, a project usually completed by several women. The completed cushions were given in 1967 and a dedication ceremony was conducted on Ascension Day, 1968.

She made them to honor her parents and in-laws. Each cushion is 18 inches in width and all were created before the altar rail was moved closer to the pulpit in the 1990s. During a robbery, a several of these were stolen. Replacement cushions were made to match by several women, the author numbered among them.

Symbols chosen are traditional in nature i.e. cross and crown, the Episcopal Church Shield, shell, Celtic cross, and fish. The kneelers were refurbished in 2010 replacing the green velvet, to a neutral color.

Stations of the Cross

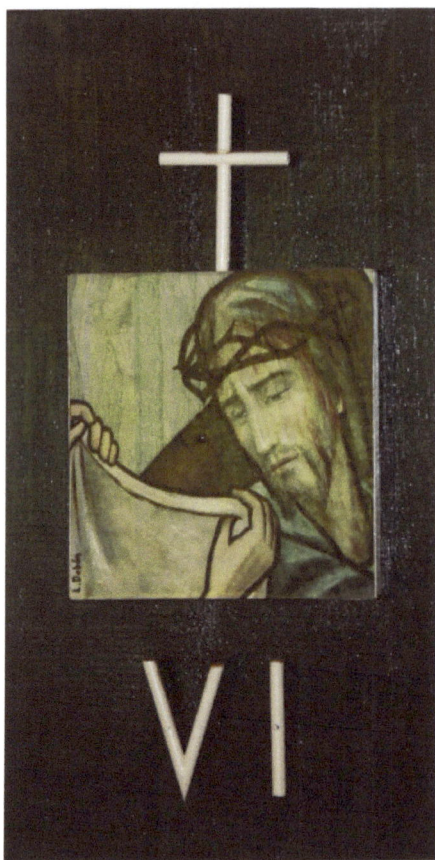

The Rev. Frank R. Alvarez wanted a set of the Stations of the Cross for the church. He and All Saints' first vocational deacon, the Rev. Daniel LePore, were on a trip to Nashotah House Seminary in Wisconsin. Fr. Alvarez was numbered among the Nashotah alumni. The prices for the desired stations sold there were beyond the funds available. Thus, the pictures were cut out from a catalogue. The original artist is unknown. Deacon LePore's brother, Dominic, prepared the wood and decoupaged the pictures, and presented these to the church in March 1974, as published in, "The Stuart News."

Sanctus Bell

This Sanctus Bell was donated in memory of Rachel Marie Smith, youngest of the two daughters of the Rev. Arthur and Mary Smith. In October 1968, Rachel Maria, age 11, passed out in the music room at the Stuart Junior High, Stuart, Florida. Her mother, Mary, was the Junior High's librarian. Fr. Smith was the Rector of St. Mary's Episcopal Church, in Stuart, down the street from that school and adjacent to the hospital in Stuart, Florida. As a U.S. Army Reserve Chaplain, Colonel Smith was away on training at the time in Georgia. The cause of Rachel's untimely death was not released publicly. Her dad, "Father Mike" Smith, started one of the first parental grief support groups in Martin County, Florida. Rachel, along with her parents, is buried in the adjoining All Saints cemetery.

Wallace and Georgia Wright Fletcher

During the tenure of the Rev. Jonathan Coffey, Sr. as the 5th Rector, the congregation was experiencing a time of great spiritual renewal. The selection of these designs and colors of these landscapes are more lively and non-traditional to reflect that time. One scene is the sunrise over the Indian River, with Florida's Hutchinson Island at the horizon; a view from the church's hilltop location. The other is an ocean view. A loggerhead turtle is included as they nest on the beaches of Martin County, Florida.

"Wally" and Georgia Fletcher, a young couple with two children, moved to All Saints from Philadelphia. As a Certified Public Accountant, he became the treasurer and senior warden repeatedly, and in his later years one of the first lay readers and chalice bearers. Georgia was behind the scenes making vestments for the priest, linens for the altar and items for sale at numerous Christmas bazaars. Georgia was instrumental in the establishment of the Bethany Ministries. This ministry included both the thrift shop and the work group, which made service items to support the visiting nurses. Their daughter, Joyce, designed the petit point cushions and stitched them in less than three years. Donated in the early 1980s, her parents were alive to enjoy seeing them in use. "Wally" and Georgia are buried along the edge of Palm Memorial Drive in the 1933 addition to All Saints Cemetery.

Closing Thoughts

Thank you for your interest in this historic church in this tropical paradise. I hope you see the faithfulness of the people whose lives are remembered here and find their lives inspirational. This is an active living church - a place to share the joys and sad events of life; a place of faithful witness to the love of God. Come and see for yourself.

Our family had no large extended family. My research of these people who are my church family and yours, left us a rich heritage. What a blessing researching this book has been!

More information on all of these memorials will be in the companion detailed history book. Publication of that effort is projected to be ready in time for the 115th anniversary of the dedication of the church. Kindly share additional information and corrections with me by writing me in care of the Parish Office at 2303 NE Seaview Drive, Jensen Beach, Florida 34957.

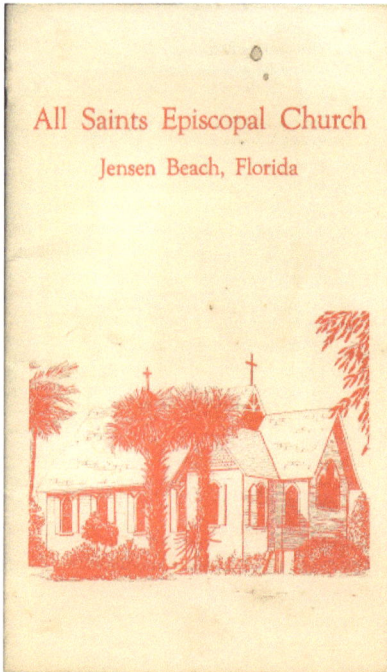

All Saints Episcopal Church
Jensen Beach, Florida

Above: 1975 Parish Telephone Directory

Right: 1933 Cemetary Addition
- c. 1960 - Top
- c. 1990 - Bottom

Glossary

An Episcopal Dictionary of the Episcopal Church> A User-Friendly Reference for Episcopalians informs descriptions found here.

Baptistery – The place in the church building where the sacrament of baptism is administered.

Bishop's Committee - The Bishop's Committee is a group of lay people, elected from and by the congregation. The group acts as representatives and leaders who oversee the business life of a church and is responsible to the Bishop.

Confirmation – The sacrament of the church where an individual affirms the baptismal vows made for them as an infant.

Holy Communion – A sacrament of the church consisting of bread and wine, which has been blessed, and is an outward and visible sign of God's grace to the people.

Diocese – A diocese is a geographical jurisdiction of the Bishop.

Junior Warden - Traditionally a position of the Vestry or Bishop's Committee, known as the people's warden; generally responsible for the care and maintenance of the church's buildings and grounds.

Mission – A congregation that is not self-supporting is known as a mission.

Parish - A congregation that is self-supporting is known as a parish.

Rector – Priest in charge of a self-supporting congregation

Rectory – The rectory is the residence of the Rector. All Saints provided this housing.

Sacristy – The room used by the clergy and all who prepare the church for the worship services of the congregation. The priest will robe in this room as well.

Senior Warden - Traditionally a position of the Vestry or Bishop's Committee, known as the priest's warden; generally responsible as a liaison between the people and the priest.

Vestry – A vestry serves as the board that manages the business of the church and has the legal responsibility for the corporate property of the church.

Vicar – In the Episcopal Church, the title generally applies to the priest in charge of a mission congregation. "Though the use the terms Vicar and Rector are not consistently used throughout the Episcopal Church," they are used in with this publication with these traditional definitions.

Vicarage – The vicarage is residence of the Vicar. All Saints provided this housing.

References and Resources

- Books by Sandra Henderson Thurlow -
    - Sewall's Point: The history of a peninsular community on Florida's Treasure Coast, Southeastern Printing, Stuart, FL, 1992
    - Historic Jensen and Eden on Florida's Indian River, Southeastern Printing, Stuart, FL, 2004
- History of Martin County, ed. Janet Hutchinson, Martin County Historical Society, Gilbert Bar Press, Hutchinson Island, FL 1975
- "An Episcopal Dictionary of the Episcopal Church> A User-Friendly Reference for Episcopalians" Don S. Armentrout, Robert Boak Slocum, editors."
- "Parish Register" Arranged by Right Reverend William Paret, Bishop of Maryland, Sixth Edition, Baltimore: The Falconer Company, 1902. This information is recorded by the clergy at the time
- "The Canonical Church Register for MISSIONS – COMPILED WITH REFERENCE TO The Canons of the Church in the United States of America, Milwaukee; The Young Churchman Company" as recorded by various unidentifiable people
- All Saints Cemetery Records
- The Stuart News, The Jensen Beach Mirror
- Websites - www.newspaperarchive.com, www.genealogybank.com, www.ancestry.com and www.findagrave.com
- Unpublished works found in the files of the All Saints-
    - "Stained Glass Windows of All Saints Episcopal Church: As of December 1977" Edward Pettit
    - Oral History by Janet Kempf Siddons – 1988

-

9 781621 371816